AMANA!—that is a name that has spelled "good food" for many years to persons who come to visit and dine in the seven villages that comprise the Amana Society in east central Iowa. Now for the first time the recipes for typical Amana dishes have been compiled into this book by the Ladies Auxiliary of the Homestead Welfare Club. While the original recipes were meant to be served in the separate community kitchens to thirty or more people who always came hurriedly and hungrily when the big bell in the steeple chimed the dinner hour, the recipes in this book have been scaled down to fit one-family appetites. The recipes are of a wide variety—the substantial everyday main dishes and the dainty, fancy cookies baked only at Christmastime, the dishes whose principal ingredient is the potato grown in abundance on the "home acres" and dishes concocted from the fragrant spices, fruits and nuts of the Orient, the dishes prepared by the ancestors of present day Amana cooks several hundred years ago in Europe and the dishes developed by some bright young matron to take full advantage of the abundant Iowa harvests.

It is our hope that you will find many of the following recipes so enjoyable that they will become your favorites—they are ours!

LADIES AUXILIARY
Homestead Welfare Club

TABLE OF CONTENTS

A BRIEF HISTORY

The history of the Amana Society begins in the year 1714 in the province of Hesse near what is now Frankfort, Germany. In that year, E. L. Gruber, a Lutheran clergyman, and J. F. Rock, together with others who shared their belief that God could and would reveal His wishes by prophecies through persons inspired as in Biblical days, organized. This sect flourished as long as Rock and Gruber were alive but declined after their death. It was revived by new leadership in the early nineteenth century at which time large estates in the relatively tolerant province of Hesse were leased as a home for the colony. The community prospered; but even in Hesse, religious and political persecution became very intense. Then, through a divine testimony the Inspirationists learned that they were to seek a new home in America. A committee of four men, among them Christian Metz, arrived in New York in October, 1842. After three months' deliberation these men bought the 5000-acre Seneca Indian Reservation near Buffalo, New York. When the colony was organized as the Ebenezer Society in 1843, about eight hundred of the Inspirationists had already come to New York. Later an additional five thousand acres was purchased, but still more was needed to satisfy the demands of the Society. However, Buffalo was growing rapidly and land prices were becoming more and more exorbitant. The leaders once more looked westward for a location with more land, and also to escape the encroaching wordly Buffalo. In 1854, a group headed by Christian Metz went to look over some of the then newly-opened government lands, first in what is now Kansas, and then in Iowa. A site along the Iowa River seemed very suitable to them and when another group returned to Iowa, they bought 18,000 acres of land in a single tract along both sides of the Iowa River in Iowa County. During the ten years of moving the community to Iowa, the Ebenezer holdings were liquidated and the Iowa land holdings were increased to 26,000 acres. Here the community existed in a pseudo-communistic order until 1932 when the holdings were reorganized into a corporation and the community kitchens, in which the recipes of this book had been used so long and so often, were a thing of the past.

SUPPEN
(Soups)

At noontime, there was always a pot of soup bubbling on
the big hearth centering the kitchen. Sometimes it was only
a thin soup when there were filling dishes on the menu; at
other times the soup was a meal in itself, especially when
there was little time to prepare a whole meal as on special
church holidays when everyone attended both morning and
afternoon services. But soup there was, made in the same
kettle day after day, a custom which seemed to give the
kettle a special flavor which it imparted to the soup.

FLEISCH BRÜHE
(Soup Stock)

1 lb. boiling beef   Parsley
2 qts. water   Leek
2 tablespoons salt   Celery
         Carrot

Tie parsley, leek, celery and carrot together, add to other ingredients and cook until meat is tender. Strain. Add any of the following ingredients to the soup stock and simmer until tender:

Rice Soup: ¾ cup rice

Noodle Soup: ½ pkg. fine noodles

Barley Soup: ¾ cup barley

Vegetable Soup: ¾ cup diced carrots

         ½ cup diced potatoes

         1 cup shredded cabbage

         ½ cup sliced celery

         ¼ cup sliced leek tops

PFANNKUCHEN SUPPE
(Pancake Soup)

2/3 cup flour
1 teaspoon baking
powder

1/2 teaspoon salt
2 eggs, separated
1 cup milk
2 tablespoons shortening

Mix flour, baking powder and salt. Add milk to slightly beaten egg yolks and add to dry ingredients. Beat until smooth, then fold in stiffly beaten egg whites. Melt shortening in heavy skillet, pour in 1 cup of the batter and fry till pancake is golden brown on both sides, turning only once. Continue likewise with rest of batter, then spread pancakes on large platter to cool. When thoroughly cold, roll up and slice in thin strips as for fine noodles. Cook in beef stock, bouillon or chicken broth for about five minutes.

RINDFLEISCH EXTRACT
(Extract of Beef)

1 lb. lean beef

Seasoning

Cut meat in small cubes and place in pint glass jar; screw top on tight. Set jar in saucepan of cold water and cover. Let simmer for 3 or 4 hours. Drain off liquid in jar, season to taste and serve.

❖❖❖
SOUPS
❖❖❖

TAUBEN SUPPE
(Pigeon Soup)

3 pigeons
3 quarts water
1 tablespoon salt
1 sprig parsley

1 cup rice, uncooked
2 eggs
½ cup sweet cream

Clean pigeons and soak in cold water for ½ hour. Chill overnight. Bring water to boil, add salt, parsley and pigeons. Boil till meat is tender, then remove from liquid and set aside to cool. Add rice to broth and cook until tender. Add meat cut in small pieces. Lastly, add eggs beaten with cream. Serve.

VERLORENE SUPPE
(Crumb Soup)

6 cups beef broth
1 cup coffee cake crust
   crumbs

2 eggs
Dash of nutmeg
Parsley

Mix crumbs into one beaten egg, add nutmeg and stir mixture into boiling broth. Bring to boil again. Beat second egg into soup tureen, slowly add hot soup and parsley sprigs.

GRIES SUPPE
(Farina Soup)

3 tablespoons butter	1 teaspoon salt
4 tablespoons farina	1 quart boiling water
1 tablespoon flour	1 egg yolk, beaten

Melt butter, add farina and flour and brown until golden in color, stirring constantly. Stir into rapidly boiling salted water and then simmer slowly for 20 minutes. Remove from heat, cool slightly, then add beaten egg yolk. Stir well and serve.

KLÖSSEL SUPPE
(Dumpling Soup)

4 tablespoons butter or vegetable shortening	¼ teaspoon nutmeg
2 eggs, separated	2½ cups bread or coffee cake crumbs
½ teaspoon salt	1 quart beef broth
1 tablespoon parsley, minced	

Cream the butter, add egg yolks, salt, parsley, and nutmeg and mix well. Add the crumbs and beaten egg whites. With hands dipped in flour, roll dough into little balls the size of a walnut. Cook slowly, uncovered, in beef broth for 10 minutes. May also be cooked in pea or rice soup.

✦✦✦

SOUPS

✦✦✦

GERÖSTE KRÜMMEN SUPPE
(Browned Crumb Soup)

1 cup flour
2 eggs, separated
1 quart boiling water

Salt to taste
2 tablespoons butter
¼ cup dry bread crumbs

Mix flour and unbeaten egg whites with fork until mixture resembles small peas. Sprinkle into boiling salted water and boil about two minutes. Brown bread crumbs in melted butter, add to soup and reheat. Remove from heat and add beaten egg yolks.

LINSEN SUPPE
(Lentil Soup)

1 cup lentils
8 cups water
1 potato, diced
2 carrots, diced or sliced
1 onion, minced
2 tablespoons butter

½ cup sliced celery
1 lb. Amana Pork
Sausage
Salt to taste
2 tablespoons flour

Soak lentils in water overnight, then cook until tender, adding more water if necessary. Add next six ingredients and cook about 20 minutes. Remove sausage and cool. Melt butter, blend in flour and add to soup as thickening. Skin sausage, slice, and add to soup. Reheat and serve.

AMANA COLONY RECIPES

RAHM SUPPE
(Cream Soup)

3 tablespoons butter
4 medium-sized bread
   heels, cubed

3 cups rich milk or
2 cups cream and
1 cup water

1 teaspoon salt

Melt butter in heavy saucepan, add bread cubes and toast over low heat until golden brown, stirring frequently to prevent scorching. Add milk and salt. Simmer for about 10 minutes over low heat. Serve hot.

KARTOFFEL SUPPE
(Potato Soup)

2 cups diced raw potatoes
1 small onion or leek
4 cups water
½ tablespoon salt

½ cup bread cubes
2 tablespoons butter
2 tablespoons cream
Pinch of pepper

Cook potatoes and onion in salted water until tender, force through sieve and return to fire. Brown bread cubes in butter and pour into boiling soup. Remove from fire, add cream and pepper and serve.

✚✚
SOUPS
✚✚

BAUMWOLLE SUPPE
(Cotton Soup)

1 tablespoon butter	2 quarts beef stock or
1 tablespoon flour	chicken broth, heated
2 eggs	

Melt butter over low heat and blend in flour. Remove from heat and stir until cold. Beat in eggs, one at a time, and add the hot broth slowly, stirring all the time. Let stand for one hour and reheat for serving.

RIEBEL SUPPE
(Riebel Soup)

1½ quarts boiling water	1 tablespoon butter
1 tablespoon salt	1½ tablespoons dry
1 egg white, unbeaten	bread crumbs
1 cup flour	

Rub flour into egg white until mixture is flaky and dry. Add slowly to boiling salted water, stirring constantly. Boil 5 minutes, then add bread crumbs browned in butter.

HAUPT SPEISEN
(Main Dishes)

Most of the meat used in the community kitchens came freshly slaughtered or home-cured from the meat markets found in all the villages, and each kitchen had its own flock of chickens to be eaten as fryers or to lay the eggs. Sometimes the woods or streams yielded up the main dish for always it was the foods at hand that were incorporated into the menus. Even the flour used in so many of the main dishes was milled in either one of the two Amana mills. However, nothing was wasted, not even things of which there was an abundance and nowhere is this so apparent as in those dishes that feature a topping of dried leftover bread crumbs toasted in butter or lard.

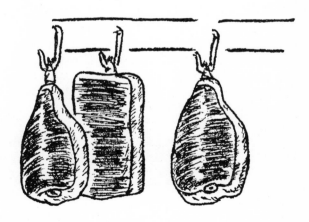

FÜLLSEL ZU GEBRATENEN HÜHNER
(Dressing for Fried Chicken)

Chicken giblets
Water to cover
1 cup sliced onions
¼ cup lard

3 slices bread soaked in
    water
Salt and pepper
Dash of nutmeg, if desired

Cook giblets until soft. Drain, saving liquid, and put through food chopper. Fry onions in lard until cooked through. Squeeze bread dry and crumble into mixing bowl. Add fried onions, ground giblets, salt and pepper. Moisten with liquid. Mix and drop by tablespoons into chicken gravy. Heat thoroughly, and serve with chicken.

NUDELN
(Noodles)

2 eggs
6 tablespoons water

1 teaspoon salt
Flour

Stir sufficient flour into slightly beaten eggs and water to make a stiff dough. Knead thoroughly, divide into two portions and roll out as thin as possible. Cover with a cloth and leave until partly dry. Then roll and cut in half-inch strips. Part of the dough may be cut very fine to be used as topping on the cooked noodles.
Boil noodles in salt water until tender. Drain. Brown ½ cup finely cut noodles in butter and pour over the cooked noodles before serving.

GEFÜLLTE NUDELN
(Filled Noodles)

1 egg	½ teaspoon salt
2 tablespoons water	¾ cup flour
	Egg white

Beat egg and water together; then add salt and sifted flour to make a fairly stiff dough. Roll out on floured surface, being careful not to roll too thin so dough won't break. Mark half of dough round lightly into 3-inch squares, brush entire round with egg white and fill with any of the following fillings:

SPINAT FÜLLSEL
(Spinach Filling)

2 lbs. chopped, raw spinach	1½ cups dry bread crumbs
3 tablespoons butter	Salt and pepper
2 eggs	2 tablespoons butter

Steam and brown spinach in melted butter; then add eggs, 1 cup of the crumbs, seasoning and mix well. Spoon this mixture onto the marked-out noodle half, putting a mound into each square. Fold over other half and seal the edges. Press dough together between mounds, both lengthwise and crosswise and then cut apart along these lines. Drop the filled squares into boiling, salted water and cook for 8 minutes or until noodles are tender. When done, lift carefully with straining spoon into serving dish and top with remaining crumbs which have been browned in butter.

MAIN DISHES

RINDFLEISCH FÜLLSEL
(Beef Filling)

1 cup ground beef	1 cup bread cubes
2 tablespoons fat	which have been
1 small onion	soaked in water
Salt and pepper	and pressed dry
⅛ teaspoon nutmeg	½ cup dry bread crumbs

2 tablespoons butter

Brown meat in hot fat; then add onion and seasonings. Remove from heat and add bread cubes. Spoon mixture onto noodle round, seal, and cook as with Spinach Filling. Top with browned bread crumbs.

HÜHNER FÜLLSEL
(Chicken Filling)

1 egg	2 teaspoons minced
⅛ teaspoon paprika	parsley
½ teaspoon salt	½ cup dry bread
1 cup, diced, cooked	crumbs
chicken	2 tablespoons butter

1 cup bread crumbs which
have been soaked in
water and pressed dry

Beat egg and seasonings together; add chicken, crumbs and parsley. Spoon mixture onto noodle round, seal, and cook as with Spinach Filling. Top with browned bread crumbs.

GEKOCHTE HASEN ODER EICHHÖRNCHEN
(Stewed Rabbit or Squirrel)

1 squirrel or rabbit,
    dressed, washed and
    cut into servings
4 tablespoons butter
6 medium-sized onions,
    sliced

1 tablespoon salt
⅛ teaspoon pepper
A few peppercorns
1½ cups water
1 teaspoon vinegar

Put layers of meat in heavy pan or skillet. Add 2 tablespoons of the butter, onions, salt, pepper, peppercorns and water and cook slowly over low heat until meat is tender. Add vinegar and remaining butter and cook two minutes longer.

POT PIE MIT SPAETZLE
(Pork and Sausage Fricassee with Dumplings)

8 pork loin ribs
8 cups water
4 medium potatoes, cut in
    half

1 lb. Amana pork sausage,
    cut in 1-inch pieces

1 recipe Spaetzle

Cook pork chops in water for one-half hour; then add potatoes and sausage and cook until potatoes are almost done. Cut well-beaten spaetzle dough into the boiling mixture and continue to cook for seven minutes.

MAIN DISHES

SPAETZLE
(Spaetzle)

1 cup milk	6 cups boiling water
2½ cups flour	1 teaspoon salt
2 eggs	4 tablespoons butter
1 teaspoon salt	½ cup dry bread crumbs

Add milk to flour slowly, stirring constantly to keep mixture smooth. Add one egg at a time, beating well after each addition. Add salt and mix well. Into separate kettle, pour boiling water, add salt and set over low heat so water is kept at simmer. Pour batter into a shallow bowl, tilt it over kettle and with a sharp knife slice batter into boiling water, being sure to dip knife into water before each slice to prevent batter from sticking to knife. Let boil for five minutes, then drain in colander. Put in serving dish and top with crumbs which have been browned in butter. Serve hot, with apple sauce.

LEBER ROLLE
(Liver Roll)

1 lb. beef liver, ground	⅛ lb. fat pork steak
1 cup bread crumbs	(ground)
2 eggs, slightly beaten	1 onion, minced
¾ teaspoon salt	1 cup milk

Mix thoroughly. Bake in loaf pan in moderate oven (350 degrees) for 1½ hours. Serve in slices.

LEBER KLÖSSE
(Liver Dumplings)

1 lb. liver, ground
½ lb. pork, ground
1 cup coffee cake or
bread crumbs
1 cup bread soaked in
water and pressed
dry
1 egg

1 scant cup flour
Salt and pepper
¼ teaspoon grated
nutmeg
1 onion, minced
Few sprigs parsley,
chopped, if desired
4 tablespoons butter

½ cup dry bread crumbs

Mix first 10 ingredients in order given and drop by teaspoons into boiling salted water. Boil 15 minutes. Remove to serving dish and top with bread crumbs which have been browned in butter.

HÜHNER SOSZE
(Creamed Chicken)

½ chicken
2 quarts water

Salt
Pinch of nutmeg

¼ cup flour

Cook chicken in salted water until tender. Remove bones and cut into small pieces. Bring one quart broth to boil and stir in flour made into paste with cold chicken broth. Cook until it thickens, then add pieces of chicken and nutmeg. If desired, ¼ cup cream and 1 beaten egg yolk may be added. The last ingredients will make it a very rich sauce.

❖❖

MAIN DISHES

❖❖

WIENER SCHNITZEL ODER KARBONADE
(Cutlets)

Veal or pork cutlets	1 egg
Salt and pepper	2 tablespoons milk
Cracker crumbs	

Wipe cutlets, sprinkle with salt and pepper. Dip into egg beaten with milk, then into finely rolled cracker crumbs. Fry slowly in deep, hot fat until brown.

VARIATION

Beef or pork cutlets	1 egg, beaten
Salt and pepper	Cracker crumbs
½ cup water	

Wipe cutlets, sprinkle with salt and pepper. Dip into beaten egg, then into finely rolled cracker crumbs. Fry in drippings until nicely browned. Put in heavy skillet, add water and cover. Simmer gently until tender, adding small amounts of water from time to time so as to make a nicely browned gravy.

SPECKEIER
(Scrambled Ham and Eggs)

1 cup boiled ham, cut in small cubes	1 tablespoon butter
	4 eggs, beaten
Salt and pepper	

Fry ham in butter slowly. Add eggs and seasoning and cook until eggs are set. Serve at once.

****
AMANA COLONY RECIPES
****

SCHWARTEN WURST
(Pork Rind Sausage)

2 lbs. pork rinds	1 teaspoon allspice
1½ lbs. boiling beef	¼ teaspoon nutmeg
3 tablespoons salt	6 medium-sized onions

Wash rinds and put to boil in a deep kettle with water to cover. Cook beef in a separate kettle. When tender, put meat through food chopper. Return to combined broths, add seasonings and onion, and bring to boil. Serve hot with boiled potatoes, or pour into pans, chill and slice; serve with catsup. This meat may be stretched by adding 6 to 8 slices of bread, preferably crusts, chopped up with the other ingredients.

GEHIRN
(Brains)

¾ lb. beef or calf brains	½ teaspoon Worcestershire Sauce
Salt and pepper to taste	Butter to brown
3 eggs, slightly beaten	

Cover brains with cold water. Let stand 30 minutes, or until colorless, and drain. Remove thick white membrane, cover with boiling water and simmer 15 minutes. Drain. Cover with cold water and drain again. Combine with seasoning, sauce and eggs and mix well. Brown in butter, turning frequently with a fork, until eggs are cooked. Diced Pimiento may be added for color.

MAIN DISHES

SAUERBRATEN
(Sauerbraten)

4 lbs. bottom round beef	2 tablespoons flour
1 cup vinegar	2 teaspoons salt
2 cups water	Pepper
2 bay leaves	2 large onions
1 teaspoon mixed spices	Browned flour

Put meat, vinegar, water, bay leaves, and spices into an earthen crock and let stand in a cool place for two or three days. Baste frequently and turn over once a day. Then drain meat, saving liquid, sprinkle with flour, salt and pepper. Brown in hot fat on all sides, add marinade and onions and cover. Cook slowly for 1½ hours or until tender. Remove meat, strain liquor, and thicken with browned flour to make a rich brown gravy. Slice meat and add to gravy.

SCHWARZSAUER
(Schwarzsauer)

2 lbs. pork liver, cut in cubes	1 small onion, minced
3 tablespoons lard	2 cups water or bouillon
¼ cup flour	2 tablespoons vinegar
	1 tablespoon salt

⅛ teaspoon pepper

Fry liver in lard very slowly, add flour, onion, and cook 20 to 30 minutes. Add water or bouillon, vinegar, salt and pepper and simmer for about 10 minutes.

HERRING SALAT
(Herring Salad)

6 salt herring, cleaned
and washed
2 cups boiled beef
1 cup dill pickles

1 cup pickled beets
4 cups apples, peeled
and quartered
1 large onion

Pepper to taste

Put through food chopper, add pepper and mix. A little cream and sugar may be added.

SCHINKEN SALAT No. 1
(Ham Salad)

1 quart boiled ham, cut in
small pieces

2 cups water
1 cup vinegar

1 large onion, cut fine

Combine all ingredients and let stand over night in porcelain crock or bowl.

SCHINKEN SALAT No. 2
(Ham Salad)

1 quart boiled ham
1 large pickle
2 hard boiled eggs
½ cup celery
2 carrots

1 cup cream
¼ cup vinegar
Salt and pepper to taste
¼ teaspoon mustard
2 eggs

1 tablespoon butter

Put first five ingredients through food chopper. Boil remaining ingredients together, stirring constantly. Cool and add to ham mixture. Chill. Serve as a sandwich filling.

MAIN DISHES

KARTOFFEL SPEISEN
(Potato Dishes)

Potatoes were plentiful and so were served morning, noon and night—fried potatoes for breakfast, boiled potatoes or special dishes for dinner, and left-overs for supper. As with main dishes, toasted bread crumbs were used often as topping. The harvest of potatoes was in itself quite an occasion. Young and old turned out to gather them up as the big special plow lifted them out of the ground.

GESCHMELZTE KARTOFFEL
(Crumbed Potatoes)

1 quart potatoes
1 tablespoon butter

1 tablespoon shortening
½ cup dry bread crumbs

Peel and slice potatoes as for French fries. Boil until tender and drain well. Fry crumbs in butter and shortening until golden brown. Pour over drained potatoes and mix until potatoes are well covered with crumbs.

KARTOFFELGEMÜSE
(Potatoes in Sauce)

3 large potatoes
1 tablespoon minced leek
or onion

1 tablespoon salt
1 tablespoon flour
1 tablespoon lard

Dash of pepper

Peel potatoes and cut in quarters lengthwise. Cover with water, add leek and salt and bring to boil. When tender, do not drain. Melt lard, blend in flour, and add to potatoes. Add pepper and let simmer for about five minutes more until flour is cooked.

KARTOFFEL GUNDEN

(Mashed Potatoes with Browned Crumbs)

6 medium-sized potatoes, boiled and mashed
2 tablespoons flour
1 tablespoon salt
3 tablespoons fat
3 tablespoons dried bread crumbs

Add flour and salt to mashed potatoes and whip until light and fluffy. Heat the fat in heavy skillet. Spoon potatoes into serving dish, dipping spoon into hot fat each time so that potatoes will retain their shape. Top with bread crumbs which have been lightly browned in the remaining fat.

SCHUPFNUDELN
(Potato Croquettes)

1½ qts. boiled riced potatoes
1½ tablespoons salt
1 egg, beaten
1 scant cup flour
½ teaspoon nutmeg, if desired

Mix thoroughly. Place on lightly floured surface and with hands dipped in flour form into long inch-thick rolls. Cut into 3-inch lengths and fry in deep fat until golden brown.

❉❉❉

POTATO DISHES
❉❉❉

GEKOCHTE KARTOFFEL KLÖSSE
(Boiled Potato Dumplings)

4 cups boiled riced
  potatoes
½ cup flour
Salt and pepper to taste
2 eggs, slightly beaten

2 slices bread, cut in
  cubes
1 medium-sized onion,
  minced
2 tablespoons butter

Blend potatoes, flour and seasoning. Add eggs. Brown bread cubes and onion in butter and add. Mix well and form into dumplings. Cook in boiling, salted water five to seven minutes. Serve with onion sauce.

ZWIEBEL SOSSE FÜR KARTOFFEL KLÖSSE
(Onion Sauce for Potato Dumplings)

½ cup minced onion
3 tablespoons lard
3 tablespoons flour

3 cups water
1 tablespoon cream
Dash of vinegar

Brown onions slightly in hot fat. Add flour and stir slowly. Add water, a little at a time, to make a smooth sauce. Take from fire, add cream and vinegar. Do not overbrown onions as sauce should have a creamy color.

ROHE KARTOFFEL KLÖSSE
(Raw Potato Dumplings)

2 cups cooked potatoes,
 riced
2 cups grated raw potatoes,
 well drained
2 eggs, beaten
1 small onion, minced
Finely chopped parsley
 to taste

¾ cup flour
3 teaspoons baking
 powder
1 tablespoon salt
4 tablespoons butter
½ cup dry bread crumbs

Mix potatoes, eggs, onion and parsley. Add flour which has been sifted with baking powder and salt. Drop by table-spoons into boiling, salted water. (If mixture is too moist to drop from spoon, add more flour.) Cook covered for 10 or 12 minutes. Lift from water, place in serving dish, and top with bread crumbs which have been browned in butter.

KARTOFFEL BREI
(Whipped Potatoes)

4 cups boiled potatoes,
 mashed
1 cup scalded milk

4 tablespoons hot melted
 butter

Combine and whip till creamy.

POTATO DISHES

KARTOFFEL BALLEN
(Potato Balls)

2 cups riced potatoes
¼ cup butter
½ cup boiling water

½ cup flour
½ teaspoon salt
2 eggs

Melt butter in the boiling water in a large sauce pan. Add flour, salt and stir well. Cook until mixture leaves sides of pan, stirring constantly. Remove from heat. Add eggs one at a time beating well after each addition. Add potatoes and mix well. Drop by tablespoons into deep fat and fry until golden brown. Serve with apple sauce or other fruit.

SCHNELLER
(Round Fried Potatoes)

1 quart small round potatoes

3 tablespoons lard

Cook potatoes in their jackets. Cool, peel, and fry in the hot lard until evenly browned. Sprinkle with salt and serve.

AMANA COLONY RECIPES

ROHGERÖSTE KARTOFFEL
(Raw Fried Potatoes)

4 large potatoes   4 tablespoons lard
Salt

Peel and slice potatoes. Soak in cold water until crisp. Drain well. Heat lard in heavy iron skillet over high flame until quite hot, then add potatoes. Lower flame and fry potatoes slowly until crusty and golden brown, turning occasionally with a pancake turner. Salt. Serve very hot.

GERÖSTE KARTOFFEL
(Hashed Brown Potatoes)

3 cups finely diced
cooked potatoes
3 tablespoons flour
1/2 teaspoon minced
onion

1/3 cup cream
1 teaspoon salt
1/8 teaspoon pepper
3 tablespoons butter or
margarine

Combine all ingredients except butter. Melt butter in heavy skillet, being sure melted butter covers all of skillet. Add potato mixture, brown slowly, about twenty minutes on each side.

❖❖

POTATO DISHES
❖❖

EINFACHE ROHE KARTOFFEL KÜCHELCHEN
(Plain Raw Potato Patties)

4 large potatoes   2 teaspoons salt
Lard

Allow one large peeled potato for each serving. Grate potatoes into mixing bowl. Add salt and mix well. Fry by spoonsful in hot greased skillet, flattening out with spoon. Brown on both sides; and serve very hot with apple sauce.

ROHE KARTOFFEL KÜCHELCHEN
(Raw Potato Patties)

6 large potatoes, grated
1 medium-sized onion, if desired
3 eggs, well beaten
1 tablespoon flour
1 tablespoon fine cracker crumbs
1 teaspoon salt

Drain potatoes well in sieve by pressing out water. Put into mixing bowl and add other ingredients. Stir until well mixed. Drop by tablespoons into hot fat, smooth into patties, and fry slowly until golden brown. Serve with apple sauce.

HEISZER KARTOFFEL SALAT
(Hot Potato Salad)

1 qt. boiled, sliced potatoes (boiled with jackets)	2 tablespoons lard
	2 tablespoons flour
	½ tablespoon salt
1 medium-sized onion, minced	3 tablespoons vinegar
	Dash of pepper

2 cups water

Set sliced potatoes aside to cool. Cook onion in lard until soft, add flour and blend well. Add salt, vinegar and pepper. Stir in water, cook till thickened and pour over potatoes. Best if made ahead of time and reheated.

GRÜNE FRATZ ODER MALM
(Potato Casserole)

4 cups raw, grated potatoes	1½ teaspoons salt
	2 tablespoons lard

Drain potatoes of moisture, add salt and spread into glass pie plate which has been greased with one tablespoon lard. Spread remaining lard over top and bake in 350 degree oven for one hour or until nicely browned. Serve with apple sauce.

✠✠✠
POTATO DISHES
✠✠✠

GEMÜSE
(Vegetables)

Vegetables were grown in the kitchen gardens. The gardens could be spotted from a distance by their water taps and large wooden tubs used to water the young plants and wash the garden implements. Gardens were cared for mostly by the older women whose special duty it was to grow the vegetables which were eaten fresh or stored for winter use.

SPINAT
(Spinach)

2 lbs. raw spinach
1 pt. boiling water
¼ cup lard
¾ cup bread crumbs
1 small onion, chopped
fine

1 heaping tablespoon
flour
½ teaspoon salt
¼ teaspoon pepper
1 pt. beef broth

Cook spinach in boiling water for 5 minutes or until tender. Remove from stove and cool spinach in cold water. Squeeze out all water and run through food chopper. Heat lard over medium heat, add bread crumbs and brown until a golden brown. Stir in onion, then flour, salt and pepper. Add ground spinach and bring to boil. Add beef broth and cook until well blended.

SAUERE GRÜNE SCHNITTBOHNEN
(Sour Green Beans)

1 qt. canned sour green
beans
1 tablespoon lard
1 tablespoon flour

1 tablespoon minced
onion
Salt and pepper to
taste

Bring beans to boil. Melt lard, add flour and stir until smooth. Add onion and brown. Add to boiling beans and cook until tender. Season. As a variation, 1 cup of cooked navy beans may be added. Serve hot.

AMANA COLONY RECIPES

SCHWARZWURZELN
(Salsify or Oyster Plant)

4 cups prepared salsify   Rich cream sauce

To prepare salsify, wash, scrape and cut into 2-inch pieces. (To prevent discoloration, soak scraped pieces in sour milk or buttermilk until ready to cook.) Cook, covered, in small amount of salted water about 20-25 minutes or until tender. Prepare rich cream sauce, add cooked salsify, heat again and serve.

TOMATEN GEMÜSE
(Stewed Tomatoes)

1 cup coffee cake cubes   ½ tablespoon salt
¼ cup butter   1 qt. tomatoes, peeled
2 tablespoons sugar   and quartered

Brown coffee cake cubes in butter, add remaining ingredients and cook for 10 minutes.

GEKOCHTER MEERRETTIG
(Boiled Horse-radish)

2 tablespoons butter   ¼ cup raw, grated
¼ cup coffee cake   horse-radish
  crumbs   Salt to taste
2 teaspoons flour   1½ cups beef broth

Melt butter in saucepan, add crumbs and brown lightly. Blend in flour and add horse-radish. Stir well, add salt and beef broth and cook for five minutes. Serve with boiled beef.

✛✛

VEGETABLES
✛✛

KERN BOHNEN
(Navy Beans)

3 cups Navy beans
6 cups water
½ lb. bacon or salt
  pork, diced
4 tablespoons brown
  sugar

2 cups tomato juice
2 tablespoons molasses
1 onion, minced
Salt and pepper to
  taste

Add water to beans and soak overnight. Boil rapidly for half an hour. Add bacon or salt pork and cook until beans are tender. Add remaining ingredients and simmer gently until well blended. Catsup may be added if desired.

GESCHMELZTE BOHNEN
(Crumbed Beans)

2 cups Navy beans
4 cups water
1 tablespoon salt
1 small onion, minced

2 tablespoons flour
2 tablespoons lard
2 tablespoons bread
  crumbs

2 tablespoons butter

Wash beans and soak overnight in the four cups water. Add salt and onion and cook until tender. Brown flour in melted lard, add to beans and simmer 10 minutes. Pour into serving dish and top with bread crumbs which have been browned in butter.

✠✠
AMANA COLONY RECIPES
✠✠

WEISSE RÜBEN
(Turnips)

6 or 8 medium-sized
turnips
1 medium potato
2 tablespoons lard
1 small minced onion
2 tablespoons flour

1 tablespoon brown
sugar
2 cups water or pork
broth
Salt and pepper to
taste

Cook turnips and potatoes until tender. Mash thoroughly in cooking water. Brown onion in lard, add flour and blend. Add turnip mixture and remaining ingredients and cook a few minutes longer.

GELBE RÜBEN
(Carrots)

2 tablespoons lard
1 medium onion,
minced
6 large carrots

2 medium potatoes
1 tablespoon sugar
Salt and pepper to
taste

Heat lard, add onion and blend well. Add carrots, potatoes and enough water to cook. When tender, take out potatoes and mash. Return to carrots, add sugar and seasoning, and cook several minutes longer. If more thickening is desired, a little flour may be added.

VEGETABLES

SAUER KRAUT
(Sour Kraut)

1½ gals. finely shredded   1 teaspoon sugar
    white cabbage   2 tablespoons salt

Mix all ingredients thoroughly in large bowl. Mash with potato masher until juice collects. Cover bowl with cloth and let stand for two hours. Then press kraut into three sterilized quart jars as firmly as possible and fill with the liquid collected in bowl. Fit screw tops loosely so the kraut can ferment and let stand at room temperature for several days. Press down again; and if necessary, make a weak salt solution, about ½ cup salt to 1 quart water, to fill jars with liquid. Screw tops on tight and store in cool place. Ready to use in about four weeks. May be eaten raw, as a relish, just as it comes from the jar or as:

Plain Cooked Sour Kraut

2 cups sour kraut   2 tablespoons lard
Water to cover   Caraway seed, if desired

Cook all together 15 minutes or longer.

Cooked Sour Kraut and Potato

2 cups cooked sour   1 medium raw potato,
    kraut   grated

Add potato to sour kraut and cook 10 minutes longer.

KRAUT GEMÜSE
(Colony Cabbage)

1 medium head of
   cabbage
2 tablespoons lard
1 medium-sized onion,
   diced

2 tablespoons flour
2 cups meat stock or
   cooking liquid
Salt and pepper to
   taste

Cut leaves from head of cabbage, break into pieces and
cook in boiling, salted water until tender. Drain, saving the
liquid if meat stock is not available. Melt lard, add onion
and fry until golden brown. Add meat stock or cooking
liquid and bring to a boil, stirring continually. Add cabbage and cook a few minutes longer. Add seasoning.

ROT KRAUT
(Red Cabbage)

2 tablespoons lard
1 medium-sized red
   cabbage (4 cups
   shredded)
2 medium-sized apples,
   chopped

1 cup water
3 tablespoons vinegar
2 tablespoons flour
3 tablespoons sugar
Salt and pepper to
   taste

Melt lard, add cabbage, apples and water and cook until
tender. Add blended flour and vinegar, sugar and seasoning and cook a few minutes longer.

❖❖❖

VEGETABLES

❖❖❖

SALATEN
(Salads)

During the winter months, relishes such as beets or pickled green tomatoes often had to suffice as a salad, but when spring came tender, green leaf lettuce grown so carefully in hotbeds was the first of the leafy salads prepared with a simple dressing that were served all through the growing season. This dressing used for nearly all salads was made with sour cream, vinegar, salt, pepper, and minced onion or onion tops mixed together according to taste.

GURKEN SALAT
(Cucumber Salad)

4 medium-sized cucum-
bers, peeled and
sliced
1 onion cut fine

2 hard boiled eggs,
sliced
½ teaspoon salt
Pepper to taste
2 tablespoons vinegar
½ cup cream

Mix all ingredients together and serve.

TOMATEN SALAT
(Tomato Salad)

6 tomatoes, skinned and
quartered
1 large onion, cut in
rings

2 tablespoons sugar
2 tablespoons vinegar
½ teaspoon salt
Dash of pepper

Mix in order given and chill.

SELLERIE SALAT
(Celery Salad)

1 bunch celery, sliced
Water to cook
½ teaspoon salt

2 tablespoons vinegar
Dash of pepper
¼ cup cream

Cook celery until tender, drain and combine with remaining
ingredients. Chill and serve.

KRAUT SALAT
(Cabbage Salad)

1 medium head of cabbage	Dash of pepper
1 onion, cut fine	2 tablespoons vinegar
½ teaspoon salt	½ teaspoon lard
	¼ cup cream

Shred cabbage fine, add onion, salt and pepper and toss. Heat vinegar and lard and pour over cabbage. Add cream and mix.

SENF SOSZE FÜR SALAT
(Mustard Sauce for Salads)

1 cup vinegar	1 teaspoon dry mustard
¾ cup sugar	¼ teaspoon pepper
2 tablespoons flour	½ teaspoon salt

3 eggs

Bring vinegar to boil. Beat remaining ingredients together with egg beater, add to vinegar and beat well. Boil a few seconds and, if desired, add a little cream. Cool. When ready to serve, add more plain or whipped cream. Especially good served over fresh sliced tomatoes.

�܁✚✚✚

SALADS
✚✚✚

GELBER BOHNEN SALAT
(Yellow Bean Salad)

1 qt. yellow beans	2 hard boiled eggs,
2 qts. boiling, salted	sliced
water	

Wash and slice beans lengthwise. Cook in salted water until tender; drain and cool. Combine with eggs and add one of the following dressings:

Hot Dressing

1 tablespoon butter	½ teaspoon salt
1 tablespoon minced	Dash pepper
onion	1 tablespoon vinegar
½ tablespoon flour	½ cup water

Brown onions in butter, blend in flour, add remaining ingredients and boil one minute. Pour over beans and eggs, mix well and serve.

Cold Sour Cream Dressing

¼ cup thick, or slightly	2 tablespoons vinegar
soured, cream	½ teaspoon salt
Dash of pepper	

Mix well and pour over beans and eggs. Chill and serve.

ENDIVIE SALAT
(Endive Salad)

1 qt. shredded endive,
    washed and drained
¼ cup vinegar
¼ cup water

½ tablespoon salt
Dash of pepper
1 tablespoon lard
1 cup sour cream

1 small onion, minced

Combine vinegar, water, seasoning and lard and bring to a boil. Remove from heat and pour over shredded endive. Let stand for several minutes, then add sour cream and onion and serve.

KNOLLEN SELLERIE SALAT
(Celeriac Salad)

4 Celeriac (roots)
Water to cook
1 tablespoon lard
1 small onion, minced

1 tablespoon flour
½ teaspoon salt
1½ tablespoons vinegar
Dash of pepper

½ cup water

Wash celeriac, cut in quarter-inch slices and cook until tender. Drain. Brown onion in lard, blend in flour, add remaining ingredients and bring to boil. Pour over celeriac and serve hot.

❖❖❖❖❖❖❖❖❖❖❖❖❖❖❖❖❖❖❖❖❖❖❖❖❖❖❖❖❖❖❖❖❖❖❖❖

SALADS

❖❖❖❖❖❖❖❖❖❖❖❖❖❖❖❖❖❖❖❖❖❖❖❖❖❖❖❖❖❖❖❖❖❖❖❖

ZIGORRIE SALAT
(Dandelion Salad)

1 qt. prepared dandelion
   greens
2 tablespoons lard or
   bacon drippings
1 tablespoon flour

1 cup water
2 tablespoons vinegar
Salt and pepper to
   taste
½ cup sour cream

Minced onion or chives, if desired

Use only young tender dandelion plants; discard roots and green tips which have a bitter taste. Cut remainder into small pieces and wash thoroughly. Soak in cold water for half an hour.. Heat lard and blend in flour. Add water and bring to boil. Season with vinegar, salt and pepper and remove from fire. Add sour cream and onion and pour over drained dandelion greens. Mix well and serve warm.

RETTIG SALAT
(Radish Salad)

2 bunches radishes
1 tablespoon salt, scant
½ cup sour cream
1 tablespoon vinegar

Dash of pepper
1 tablespoon minced
   chives

Wash radishes and slice thin or grate fine. Add salt, mix well and let stand for ½ hour. Drain off liquid and add remaining ingredients. Mix well and serve cold.

✢✥✢
AMANA COLONY RECIPES
✢✥✢

MEHLSPEISEN UND EINFACHE NACHTISCHE
(Plain Desserts)

Well-rounded meals included desserts of many varieties. There might be pie or cake, but dishes such as bread pudding or apple fritters appeared far more frequently. Most of these desserts were made from ingredients which were readily available as well as inexpensive. In fact, not a few were made of leftovers, particularly cake or yeast cake. Since many were made with flour or flour products, they were commonly referred to as "Mehlspeisen" or flour-dishes.

APFEL KÜCHELCHEN
(Apple Fritters)

½ cup flour
¼ teaspoon salt
6 tablespoons milk
2 eggs, separated

2 tablespoons sugar
4 apples, peeled and
cored

Sift flour, sugar and salt; add milk and egg yolks and beat well. Beat egg whites until stiff and fold into first mixture. Cut each apple into four rings and dip each ring into this batter, then fry in deep fat until nicely browned. Serve with the following sauce.

Sauce

2 cups milk
3 tablespoons flour

1 egg
½ cup sugar
Pinch of salt

Scald 1½ cups milk. Blend flour with remaining milk and add rest of ingredients. Add to scalded milk and cook for 15 minutes in top of double boiler. Serve hot.

SCHNEE KÜCHLEIN No. 1
(Fritters)

½ cup flour
⅜ cup milk

½ teaspoon sugar
¼ teaspoon salt
2 eggs (separated)

Mix flour and salt. Add milk and egg yolks, and beat well. Beat egg whites until stiff. Add sugar and beat. Fold into first mixture and fry in deep fat until golden brown. Serve immediately.

SCHNEE KÜCHLEIN No. 2
(Fritters)

6 eggs, separated   6 tablespoons milk
6 tablespoons flour

Mix beaten egg yolks and milk; add flour and beat until smooth. Fold in stiffly beaten egg whites. Drop by table-spoonsful into deep fat and fry until golden brown. Sprinkle with powdered sugar and serve.

PFÜTTEL
(Puffs)

2 cups milk   2 cups flour
3 tablespoons butter   6 eggs

Bring milk to boil, add butter and stir until melted. Add flour, all at one time, and stir quickly until mixture shrinks away from sides of pan. Cool slightly, then add eggs, one at a time, and stir well after each addition. Drop batter by teaspoons into deep, hot fat, and fry until golden brown. Drain on absorbent paper, sprinkle with powdered sugar and serve.

PLAIN DESSERTS

WINDBEUTEL
(Cream Puffs)

2 cups water   3 cups flour
½ lb. butter   8 eggs

Bring water and butter to boil; add flour, all at one time, and boil for one minute. Cool slightly, then add eggs, one at a time, and beat thoroughly. Drop by tablespoons onto greased baking sheet and bake for 15 minutes in 425 degree oven, then decrease heat to 350 degrees and bake 30 minutes longer or until well browned. When cool, cut into one side and fill with the following:

Filling

4 cups milk   2 eggs
5 tablespoons cornstarch   1 teaspoon butter
1 cup sugar   1 teaspoon vanilla

Use a bit of the milk to dissolve cornstarch. Heat remainder in top of double boiler. Add sugar, eggs, dissolved cornstarch and butter. Cook until thickened. Remove from heat and add vanilla. When cool, fill into cream puffs.

KUCHEN SCHNITTEN
(French Dessert Toast)

6 slices coffee cake or
    stale bread
1 egg, beaten
1 cup milk
¼ cup sugar

½ teaspoon vanilla, if
    desired
Dash of nutmeg
½ cup flour
Additional milk

Mix egg, milk, sugar, vanilla and nutmeg. Dip slices of coffee cake into this mixture and drain in colander; make a batter with the flour and left-over egg mixture, adding more milk if batter is too thick. Dip the drained slices into this batter and fry in inch-deep hot fat. Serve with fruit.

MÜRBE RINGE

(Baking Soda Doughnuts)

1 cup butter or lard
2 cups sugar
6 eggs

1 teaspoon baking
    soda
1¼ cups buttermilk

Flour—enough to make a stiff dough

Cream butter and sugar, add eggs and beat well. Dissolve soda in buttermilk and add with enough flour to make dough stiff enough to roll out. Cut with doughnut cutter and fry in deep fat until golden brown.

PLAIN DESSERTS

REIS MIT CITRONEN SOSZE
(Rice with Lemon Sauce)

1 cup rice	½ cup sugar
1 quart milk	Pinch of salt

Blend all ingredients and cook in top of double boiler until rice is tender. Pour into serving dish or individual dishes and chill. Serve with the following sauce.

Lemon Sauce

1 cup sugar	1½ cups boiling water
1½ tablespoons cornstarch	1 teaspoon butter
Juice of two lemons	1 egg, separated

Mix sugar, cornstarch, and lemon juice. Add boiling water and cook in top of double boiler until thick. Add butter and beaten yolk and remove from heat. When cold, add stiffly beaten egg white.

REIS PUDDING
(Rice Pudding)

½ cup rice	2 tablespoons butter
1½ cups milk	4 eggs, separated
¼ cup sugar	

Wash rice, cook with milk in top of double boiler until tender. Cool. Cream butter, egg yolks and sugar, add to cooled rice. Fold in stiffly beaten egg whites. Pour into greased baking dish and bake in 300 degree oven 45 to 60 minutes.

MEHL PUDDING
(Flour Pudding)

¾ cup butter or
   shortening
¾ cup flour

4 cups milk
1 cup sugar
9 eggs (separated)

Cut butter into flour; then add milk which has been scalded. Next add sugar, and cook mixture in top of double boiler until thick and creamy. Stir well to avoid lumping. Cool mixture to lukewarm. Then add one egg yolk at a time, beating well after each addition. Continue beating until batter is light and fluffy, then fold in stiffly beaten egg whites. Pour mixture slowly into two medium-sized greased pudding molds. Bake at 350 degrees for one hour.

GRIES PUDDING
(Farina Pudding)

2 2/3 cups milk
1/2 cup farina
1 1/2 tablespoons butter

4 eggs, separated
1/3 cup sugar
1/2 teaspoon salt

Scald milk; add farina and butter and cook in double boiler until thick. Remove from heat. When cool, add sugar and beaten yolks. Then fold in egg whites. Pour into two greased 10½ by 6½ inch baking pans and bake for about an hour at 350 degrees. It is best not to open oven door during baking time. Serve with fruit sauce.

❖❖
PLAIN DESSERTS
❖❖

GROSSE PFANNKUCHEN
(Dessert Pancakes)

1 cup flour
1 cup milk

½ teaspoon salt
2 eggs

Stir milk slowly into flour mixed with salt, making a smooth, thin batter. Add eggs, one at a time, beating after each addition. Heat and grease skillet, pour enough batter into it to cover bottom sparingly. Tilt skillet, if necessary, so batter spreads completely over bottom. Brown slowly on one side, then turn and brown on other side. Stack on serving plate, sprinkling each pancake with powdered sugar. Fruit sauce or syrup may be served with these.

KRÜMMEL PUDDING
(Crumb Pudding)

2 cups bread or coffee
    cake crumbs
4 eggs, beaten
½ cup sugar

1 quart milk
1 teaspoon vanilla or
    lemon extract

Combine ingredients and mix well. Bake in loaf pan in moderate oven (350 degrees) for 30 or 35 minutes.

SCHOKOLADE BROT PUDDING
(Chocolate Bread Pudding)

2 cups milk, scalded	1 cup bread crumbs
1 tablespoon butter	2 eggs, separated
1 square unsweetened chocolate	½ cup sugar

Melt butter and chocolate in scalded milk and pour over bread crumbs. Beat egg yolks, blend in sugar and add to crumb mixture. Fold in stiffly beaten egg whites, pour into greased casserole and bake in 350 degree oven until set.

ROTE GRÜTZE
(Fruit Tapioca)

1 cup canned fruit juice (cherry, plum or currant)	1 cup water
	3 tablespoons tapioca
	¼ cup sugar

Heat fruit juice and water, add tapioca and sugar and boil for three minutes. Pour into glass pudding mold and chill. Serve with:

Vanilla Sauce

1 egg	2 cups rich milk
½ cup sugar	1 teaspoon vanilla

Beat egg and sugar until foamy. Slowly beat in milk and vanilla. Serve very cold over fruit tapioca.

PLAIN DESSERTS

GUGELOPF
(Dessert Yeast Bread)

1 cup milk	1 cup sugar
1 cake compressed	5 eggs
yeast	4 cups flour
1 cup butter or	½ teaspoon salt
shortening	Rind of one lemon

1 teaspoon vanilla

Heat milk. Cool to lukewarm, then add yeast to dissolve. Cream butter and sugar, beat in one egg at a time. Add milk alternately with flour and salt, then lemon rind and vanilla. Pour dough into two greased loaf pans or "Gugelopf" form. Let rise until double in size (one to two hours). Bake in 350 degree oven until nicely browned.

WAFFELN ZUM NACHTISCH
(Dessert Waffles)

1 cup butter	1 cup buttermilk
2 cups sifted flour	½ teaspoon soda

6 eggs, separated

Cut butter into flour, dissolve soda in buttermilk and add to flour mixture slowly. Beat till smooth. Add egg yolks and beat well. Fold in stiffly-beaten egg whites and bake on very hot waffle iron until golden brown. Sprinkle generously with powdered sugar and serve with fruit in season, generally strawberries or cherries.

KALTER COCOA PUDDING
(Chilled Cocoa Pudding)

6 tablespoons cornstarch	2 cups cold milk
2 tablespoons cocoa	2 cups hot milk
6 tablespoons sugar	1 tablespoon vanilla

Blend cornstarch, cocoa, sugar and cold milk. Stir into hot milk and cook in top of double boiler until thick, stirring constantly. Add vanilla and pour into two pudding molds. Chill.

Vanilla Sauce

2 cups hot milk	1 tablespoon cornstarch
½ cup sugar	1 egg, well beaten
	1 teaspoon vanilla

Mix sugar, cornstarch and egg. Add to hot milk and cook for three minutes. Add vanilla. Cool and serve over chilled Cocoa Pudding.

WEIN SOSZE
(Wine Sauce)

1 1/3 cups water	1 egg
1 tablespoon cornstarch	1/4 cup sugar
	1/2 cup red grape wine

Bring one cup of the water to boil. Add cornstarch which has been blended with the remaining water and cook until clear. Add beaten egg and sugar and cook a few minutes longer. Remove from heat and add wine. Pour over coffee cake or sponge cup cakes and serve immediately.

✠✠

PLAIN DESSERTS
✠✠

KÜSS PUDDING
(Kiss Pudding)

3 eggs, separated	½ cup cold milk
1 cup sugar	3½ cups milk, scalded
3 tablespoons cornstrach	1 teaspoon vanilla

Beat egg yolks and sugar until light and foamy. Add cornstarch dissolved in cold milk. Pour slowly into scalded milk, stirring constantly. Cook in top of double boiler until thick. Fold in stiffly beaten egg whites, add vanilla and remove from heat. Serve cold with

Chocolate Sauce

½ cup sugar	2 tablespoons cocoa
1 teaspoon cornstarch	2 cups milk, scalded
2 egg yolks or 1 whole egg	

Mix dry ingredients, stir into hot milk and cook until smooth. Add eggs and cook until mixture coats a spoon. Cool and serve over Kiss Pudding.

TRAUBEN SOSZE
(Grape Sauce)

1 quart grapes	½ cup sugar
1 tablespoon cornstarch	

Wash and stem grapes, cover with water and boil until tender. Press through colander; add sugar and cornstarch. Boil until thickened. Cool and serve over pudding or French toast.

HEFENKLÖSSE MIT ZIMMETSOSZE

(Yeast Dumplings with Cinnamon Sauce)

1 cup milk	2 eggs, beaten
½ cup lard	½ cake compressed
1 tablespoon sugar	yeast
1 teaspoon salt	¼ cup warm water

4 cups sifted flour

. . .

1 tablespoon lard	¾ cup boiling water

1 teaspoon salt

. . .

2 tablespoons bread crumbs	2 tablespoons butter

Heat milk, add lard, sugar, salt and beaten eggs. When cooled to lukewarm, add yeast dissolved in warm water. Add flour. Let rise overnight in a warm place. Form dough into dumplings about two inches across and let rise again on cloth covered board till double in bulk. Into heavy skillet with tight fitting cover, put lard, boiling water and salt. Place dumplings in skillet, side by side, cover, and simmer 15 minutes without removing lid. Place in serving dish and top with bread crumbs which have been browned in butter. Serve with

Cinnamon Sauce

¾ cup sugar	2 teaspoons cinnamon
¾ cup flour	½ cup cold milk

2½ cups scalded milk

Mix sugar, flour, and cinnamon. Moisten with cold milk, add to scalded milk, and cook in top of double boiler for 20 minutes. Serve hot with Yeast Dumplings.

✤✤

PLAIN DESSERTS

✤✤

PASTETEN
(Pies)

Thursday was the children's delight for on that day the dinner dessert was always something special, often pie. What a feast for childish eyes were the rows and rows of pies, often as many as twenty, set to cool on the long dining room tables.

UNFEHLBARE PASTETENKRUSTE
(Never-fail Pie Crust)

1¾ cup sifted flour
½ teaspoon salt
½ teaspoon baking
  powder

½ cup shortening
¼ cup boiling
  water

Sift flour with baking powder and salt. With pastry blender or two knives cut in shortening, add boiling water and mix until well blended. Sometimes a little more water is required, but add only enough to make the dough hold together. Form into two balls and store overnight or several hours in refrigerator. Makes one large two-crust pie.

CITRONEN PASTETE
(Lemon Pie)

1½ cups boiling water
1½ cups sugar
  3 tablespoons corn-
    starch
  3 beaten egg yolks

2 teaspoons butter
2 lemons, juice and
  grated rind
3 egg whites
6 tablespoons sugar

Mix sugar and cornstarch; add boiling water. Cook for five minutes, then add the beaten egg yolks. Remove from heat, add butter, lemon juice and rind. When cool, pour into baked pie shell. Top with egg whites beaten with sugar and brown in moderate oven, 350 degrees, for about twenty minutes.

MÜRBE TEIG FÜR OBSTKUCHEN
(Tender Crust for Fruit Pies)

2¼ cups flour
¼ teaspoon salt
½ cup sugar
2 teaspoons baking
powder

¼ cup lard
¾ cup milk

* * *

Fruit, fresh or canned
(Peaches, apples, cherries
or plums)
1 cup sugar

1 cup thin cream
2 tablespoons flour
2 eggs

Combine flour, salt, sugar and baking powder. Cut in lard, then add milk, and form into a ball. Divide into two equal parts and roll out on floured board to fit two greased 9-inch cake tins. Arrange a layer of sliced fruit in circles on unbaked crusts. Beat remaining ingredients together and pour over fruit. Bake in hot oven, 425 degrees, for ten minutes. Then reduce heat to 350 degrees and bake until fruit is cooked and custard well set.

CUSTARD PASTETE
(Custard Pie)

4 eggs
4 cups milk

4 tablespoons sugar
½ teaspoon vanilla

Dash of nutmeg

Beat eggs, add remaining ingredients, blending well. Pour into pastry lined pie tin and bake in very hot oven, 450 degrees, for ten minutes. Then reduce heat to 325 degrees and bake about thirty minutes longer or until a knife inserted comes out clean.

❖❖❖❖❖❖❖❖❖❖❖❖❖❖❖❖❖❖❖❖❖❖❖❖❖❖❖❖❖❖❖❖❖❖❖❖
PIES
❖❖❖❖❖❖❖❖❖❖❖❖❖❖❖❖❖❖❖❖❖❖❖❖❖❖❖❖❖❖❖❖❖❖❖❖

SCHOKOLADE PASTETE No. 1
(Chocolate Pie)

2 cups sugar
4 tablespoons cornstarch
2 cups boiling water
2 ounces unsweetened
   chocolate, grated

4 egg yolks
2 tablespoons butter
4 stiffly beaten egg
   whites
½ cup sugar

Mix sugar and cornstarch, add boiling water, stirring constantly. Add chocolate, egg yolks and butter. Cook a few minutes longer. Cool. Pour into two baked pie shells and top with egg whites beaten with sugar. Bake in slow oven, 325 degrees; until meringue is golden brown.

SCHOKOLADE PASTETE No. 2
(Chocolate Pie)

2 ounces unsweetened chocolate
2 1/4 cups milk
3 eggs, separated

3/4 cup sugar
1/3 cup flour
1 teaspoon vanilla
4 tablespoons sugar

Put chocolate in milk and bring to boil. Combine ¾ cup sugar and flour and slowly stir in hot milk mixture. Add a small amount of this to beaten egg yolks; stir into remaining hot mixture. Cook until thick and creamy, stirring constantly. Remove from heat, add vanilla and cool. Pour into baked pie shell and top with meringue made from egg whites stiffly beaten with the 4 tablespoons sugar. Bake in 350 degree oven for about twenty minutes until nicely browned.

TRAUBEN PASTETE
(Two-crust Grape Pie)

3 cups grapes   Dash of salt
2/3 cup sugar   2 teaspoons lemon
3 tablespoons flour   juice
1 tablespoon melted butter

Wash grapes, separate skins from pulp and cook pulp until soft. Sieve to remove seeds, and add skins. Mix sugar, flour and salt, and combine with grapes. Add lemon juice and butter. Pour into 9-inch pastry lined pie plate. Adjust slit top crust and flute edge. Bake ten minutes in hot oven, 450 degrees. Then reduce heat to 350 degrees and bake until top crust is nicely browned.

KÜRBIS PASTETE
(Pumpkin Pie)

2 cups pumpkin, cooked   1 quart milk
     and strained   1 teaspoon cinnamon
1 cup sugar   Dash of nutmeg, mace
4 egg yolks   and ginger
4 beaten egg whites

Combine first six ingredients in order given and mix well. Then fold in beaten egg whites. Pour into unbaked pie shells and bake in 450 degree oven for ten minutes, then in 325 degree oven for forty-five minutes, or until knife inserted comes out clean. This is enough filling for two 9-inch pies.

PIES

RAHM PASTETE FÜR APFEL KRAPFEN

(Cream Pastry for Apple Dumplings)

4 cups sifted flour
3 tablespoons cold butter
  or vegetable shorten-
  ing
1 teaspoon salt

1 tablespoon sugar
1 beaten egg
1 cup sour cream
1 teaspoon soda
1 tablespoon water

. . .

Apples
Brown sugar

Cinnamon
Butter

Cut butter into flour. Mix egg, cream, salt and sugar together and add to flour. Dissolve soda in water and mix into first batter. Handling very lightly and as little as possible, roll dough into two sheets as for pie crust. Then cut into 6- or 7-inch squares. Makes about twenty squares. Peel and core as many apples as needed and put one on top of each square. Sprinkle with brown sugar, dash of cinnamon and a dab of butter. Fold corners of squares over apple and place in a greased baking dish. Sprinkle with more sugar, butter and cinnamon. Pour ¼ cup of boiling water in bottom of dish and bake in 375 degree oven until apples are soft. Serve with sweet cream, or

Brown Sugar Sauce

1 cup light brown sugar
2 tablespoons flour

2 tablespoons butter
2 cups boiling water

Boil all ingredients over slow heat until slightly thickened. Serve hot over dumplings.

KUCHEN
(Cakes and Yeast Breads)

Cake was served only on rare occasions, but the baking of yeast breads was a weekly occurrence. On Saturday mornings the fragrance of freshly baked yeast breads filled the air for that was always baking day. The crusty braided loaves were served for Sunday morning breakfast, but the round glossy buns were eaten the same day.

WEINACHTS STOLLEN
(Christmas Yeast Cake)

1 cake yeast
2 cups lukewarm
    water
4 quarts flour,
    warmed
1 tablespoon salt
3½ cups sugar

1½ cups prepared but-
    ter* or half lard,
    half butter
½ pkg. citron ,cut fine
Milk, lukewarm
1 lb. raisins
1 cup almonds or
    hickory nuts,
    chopped fine

. . .

Melted butter

1 cup sugar
1 teaspoon cinnamon

Dissolve yeast in lukewarm water, add 2 cups flour, mix well and let rise until double in bulk. Sift remaining flour into large pan together with salt and sugar. Add yeast, melted butter, citron, and enough milk to make a medium stiff dough. Knead thoroughly, add raisins and nuts and knead again until well blended. Let rise until double in bulk. Divide dough into four parts, shape each part to fit into greased cake tin or loaf pan, and let rise again until double in bulk. Just before baking, cut a deep gash down the center of each loaf. Bake in 350 degree oven about one hour. Brush with melted butter and sprinkle with cinnamon-sugar mixture.

*Simmer butter over low heat until it ceases bubbling and strain. May be used in butter cakes too. Settlings are good eaten on bread.

EWIGER HEFENTEIG
(Everlasting Dough)

1 cup milk, scalded	1 cup sugar
1 cup potato water	2 teaspoons salt
1 potato, mashed	1 cake compressed
1 cup water	yeast, dissolved
1 cup lard, melted	in a little water

8 cups flour

Mix the first eight ingredients and two cups of the flour and beat 5 minutes. Let rise in a warm place about 2 hours. Add remaining flour and store in refrigerator until ready to use.

For DOUGHNUTS, roll out ⅜ inch thick on lightly floured board and cut out with floured biscuit cutter. Put in warm place to rise until double in bulk. Press hole through each as you drop into hot fat and fry until a golden brown on both sides. Turn only once. Drain on absorbent paper and roll in granulated sugar.

This dough also may be used for fruit and streusel kuchen listed under Basic Yeast Dough.

CAKES AND YEAST BREADS

HEFENTEIG
(Basic Yeast Dough)

1 cup milk	1 cup lukewarm water
½ cup sugar	6 cups sifted flour
1 tablespoon salt	6 tablespoons melted
1 cake compressed	shortening
yeast	

Scald milk, add sugar and salt. Cool to lukewarm. Dissolve yeast in lukewarm water and add to cooled milk. Add 3 cups flour and beat until smooth. Add melted shortening and remaining flour. Knead well. Place in greased bowl, cover and set in warm place away from drafts. Let rise until double in bulk or about three hours. This dough may be shaped into twists, braids, buns, or other fancy shapes and baked at 350 degrees for about 20 minutes; or it may also be kept in the refrigerator for four to five days and portions cut off as needed.

STREUSEL KUCHEN
(Streusel Kuchen)

Basic Yeast Dough

Take part of dough about size of a small saucer and roll out on lightly floured board to ½-inch thickness and place in well- greased pie tin or 8x8-inch square pan. Let rise again until light. Prick top with fork, brush with melted butter, and sprinkle with topping made of

1/4 cup butter	1/3 cup sifted flour
1/4 cup brown sugar	1 teaspoon cinnamon

Cream butter, add sugar and mix well. Add remaining ingredients and stir until well mixed and crumbly. Sprinkle generously over prepared cake. Bake at 350 degrees for about twenty to twenty-five minutes.

NEU JAHR'S PRETZEL
(New Year's Pretzel)

½ recipe Basic Yeast Dough

Divide dough into six equal portions. Roll each portion into rope about ¼ inch thick and 12 inches long, twist into form of a pretzel and place on greased baking tin. Let rise again until light. Bake in hot oven, 425 degrees, for about twenty minutes. Ice tops while still warm with

Rose Water Icing

1 cup confectioner's sugar

4 teaspoons milk or warm water

½ teaspoon rose water

Stir together to a smooth, fairly thick paste and use at once.

OBST KUCHEN
(Fruit Kuchen)

Basic Yeast Dough
Prepared Fruit—sliced
   apples, sliced rhu-
   barb, pitted cherries,

sliced peaches, dried
   peaches, pitted plums
   may be used
1 cup sugar

Roll out dough as for streusel kuchen, place in greased pie plate, brush with butter and sprinkle with ¼ cup sugar. Press prepared fruit into dough close together. Sprinkle remaining sugar over fruit (using a bit more sugar for acid fruits like rhubarb). Let rise. Before baking, beat one egg and 2 tablespoons cream together and spoon over the fruit. Cover cake with pan and bake for ten minutes at 400 degrees, then remove pan and continue baking at same temperature for about 25 minutes more.

GEROLLTER GELEE KUCHEN
(Jelly Roll)

4 eggs, separated
½ cup sugar
½ cup flour

½ teaspoon baking
   powder

Beat egg whites until stiff. Add sugar and beat well; then add the yolks, beating constantly. Fold in flour sifted with baking powder. Bake in 8x12 inch tin at 400 degrees for 15 minutes. When done, turn out on a wet cloth, spread with jelly and roll up. Dust with powdered sugar.

❖❖

CAKES AND YEAST BREADS

❖❖

PFLAUMEN KUCHEN
(Plum Cake)

1/2 cup scalded milk	1/3 cake compressed
1/2 cup vegetable	yeast
shortening	2 eggs
1/4 cup sugar	2 cups flour

Raw plums, pitted (or canned plums, strained)

Combine milk, shortening, and sugar, and let cool to luke-warm. Dissolve yeast in this mixture and add well beaten eggs. Add flour and beat thoroughly. Let rise in refrigerator overnight. Then roll out on lightly floured board to fit into two 9x9 inch pans. Let rise until double in bulk. Arrange a layer of fruit on dough, top with crumbs, and bake for 30 minutes in 350 degree oven.

Crumb Topping

1 cup sugar	1 tablespoon flour
¼ cup butter	

Cut butter into combined flour and sugar and sprinkle over fruit.

GEFÜLLTER KUCHEN
(Cream Cake)

3 eggs
1 cup sugar
1¼ cup flour

2 teaspoons baking
powder
½ teaspoon salt

½ cup milk

Beat eggs, add sugar gradually and beat until foamy. Sift flour, baking powder and salt together and add alternately with the milk. Bake in two 8-inch greased and floured cake tins in 375 degree oven for about 25 minutes. When cool, split cake and spread the following filling between halves:

Filling

1½ cups milk, scalded
1 cup sugar
2 tablespoons corn-
starch

2 tablespoons butter
¼ teaspoon salt
½ cup cold milk
2 eggs, well beaten

2 teaspoons vanilla

Combine sugar, cornstarch, butter, salt and cold milk. Stir into scalded milk and cook in top of double boiler until thickened, stirring constantly. Slowly add the beaten eggs and cook several minutes longer. When cool, add vanilla.

CAKES AND YEAST BREADS

ZWETCHEN KUCHEN
(Prune Cake)

¾ cup butter
1 cup sugar
3 eggs, separated
3 tablespoons sour
    cream
2 cups flour, sifted twice
    before measuring

1 teaspoon soda
1 teaspoon allspice
1 teaspoon cinnamon
Speck of salt
1 cup cooked, chopped
    prunes

Cream butter and sugar; add well beaten egg yolks and blend. Add sour cream alternately with dry ingredients which have been sifted together. Add prunes and fold in stiffly beaten egg whites. Pour into 3 greased and floured cake tins and bake in 350 degree oven for 20 minutes. When cool spread following filling between layers.

Sour Cream Filling

2 eggs
½ cup sour cream
1 cup chopped cooked
    prunes

2 tablespoons butter
Pinch of salt

Combine all ingredients and cook in top of double boiler until quite thick.

ROTHER MARMOR KUCHEN
(Red Marble Cake)

White Part

½ cup butter or other shortening	3 teaspoons baking powder
1 cup sugar	5 stiffly beaten egg whites
½ cup sour cream	
2 cups flour	

Cream butter and sugar, add cream alternately with the flour which has been sifted with baking powder. Fold in egg whites.

Red Part

½ cup butter or other shortening	½ cup sour cream
1 cup red sugar	2 cups flour
5 well beaten egg yolks	2 teaspoons baking powder

Cream butter and sugar, add egg yolks and beat well. Add cream alternately with flour which has been sifted with baking powder.

Grease and flour 2 loaf pans or one large tube pan. Alternate 1 tablespoon red batter and 1 tablespoon white batter and when pan is filled run a knife through crosswise several times to give marble effect. Bake in 350 degree oven for one hour.

CAKES AND YEAST BREADS

MOHN SAMEN KUCHEN
(Poppy Seed Cake)

1/3 cup poppy seed	1 1/2 cups sugar
1 cup milk	2 cups flour
3/4 cup butter or other	2 teaspoons baking
shortening	powder

4 egg whites, stiffly beaten

Soak poppy seed in milk, preferably over night or at least several hours. Cream butter, add sugar and mix well. Sift together flour and baking powder and add alternately with the milk and poppy seed. Fold in egg whites. Bake in two layers in 375 degree oven for about 45 minutes.

Filling

4 egg yolks	2 tablespoons cornstarch
1 cup sugar	1 cup water

½ cup nut meats

Mix egg yolks, sugar and cornstarch. Add water and cook until thick. When cool, add nut meats and spread between layers. Frost with white frosting.

BISQUIT
(Biscuit Cake)

6 egg whites, stiffly
    beaten

1 cup sugar

6 eggs yolks, beaten
    until light lemon-
    colored

1 cup sifted flour

1 teaspoon vanilla

To beaten egg whites, slowly add sugar, one tablespoon at
a time, beating all the while. Add beaten egg yolks alternately with the flour, beating after each addition. Pour immediately into tube pan that has been well greased and
sprinkled with granulated sugar. Bake in slow oven (275
degrees) for one hour. Remove from pan immediately and
cool on rack.

GUTER NUSZKUCHEN
(Deluxe Nut Cake)

½ cup butter
1 cup sugar
2 eggs
2 cups flour

2 teaspoons baking
    powder
1 cup milk
1 cup chopped nuts

1 teaspoon vanilla

Cream butter, add sugar and cream until fluffy. Add eggs
and beat well. Sift together flour and baking powder and
add alternately with the milk. Add nuts and vanilla. Pour
into two greased and floured cake tins and bake 25 or 30
minutes in 325 degree oven. Frost as desired.

CAKES AND YEAST BREADS

GEWÜRZ KUCHEN
(Spice Cake)

½ cup shortening
1 cup sugar
¼ teaspoon salt
1 egg
1 cup raisins

½ teaspoon cinnamon
2 cups flour
1 cup sour milk
1 rounded teaspoon
    baking soda

Cream shortening with sugar and salt, add egg and beat well. Blend in raisins and cinnamon. Add flour alternately with sour milk in which soda has been dissolved. Blend well. Bake in loaf pan in 350 degree oven for one hour or bake in two 9-inch layer cake tins for 25 minutes.

WASSER KUCHEN
(Water Sponge Cake)

3 eggs
1 cup sugar
1 cup flour

1 teaspoon baking
    powder
½ cup water

Beat eggs until foamy; add sugar. Sift flour and baking powder and add alternately with the water. Pour into a 9x12 inch cake tin that has been greased and floured. Bake in hot oven, 375 degrees, for 20 or 25 minutes. Cut in squares and serve with vanilla or wine sauce.

KRUMMEN KUCHEN
(Crumb Cake)

2 cups brown sugar
1 tablespoon lard
2 cups flour
½ teaspoon salt

1 cup sour milk
1 teaspoon soda
2 eggs
1 teaspoon vanilla

Mix sugar, lard, flour and salt together. Take out scant cup of the mixture and set aside. To the remaining add sour milk in which the soda has been dissolved, eggs and vanilla. Mix and pour into 8½x11½ inch greased and floured cake tin, then spread the scant cup of crumbs over it and bake at 350 degrees for 25 to 30 minutes. Nuts may be added to the crumb topping if desired.

CUP CAKE
(Cup Cake)

¾ cup butter
2 cups sugar
4 eggs
1 cup milk
3 cups flour

3 teaspoons baking
  powder
1 teaspoon almond
  flavor

Cream butter, add sugar and mix well. Add eggs one at a time. Sift flour and baking powder and add alternately with the milk. Add flavoring. Bake in three layers at 375 degrees for 45 minutes. Or divide the dough and add 1/3 cup cocoa, 2 tablespoons sugar, mixed with 1/4 cup hot water to one part and bake as marble cake at 350 degrees for one hour.

❖❖
CAKES AND YEAST BREADS
❖❖

NONNEN KUCHEN
(Nun's Cake)

1 cup butter or vege-
table shortening
1½ cups powdered
sugar
5 egg yolks
2 egg whites,
unbeaten
¾ cup milk

3 cups flour
2½ teaspoons baking
powder
¾ teaspoon salt
3 teaspoons caraway
seeds
2 teaspoons rose
water

½ teaspoon extract of cinnamon

Cream butter; add sugar and egg yolks and beat well. Stir in unbeaten egg whites, beat one minute. Then add milk alternately with flour sifted with baking powder and salt. Add caraway seed; beat well and then add flavoring. Pour into 7½-inch round cake pan, 3½ inches deep. Bake in 375 degree oven for one hour and 20 minutes.

BROT TORTE
(Bread Torte)

9 eggs, separated
1 cup sugar
¼ teaspoon cloves

½ teaspoon cinnamon
1 cup sifted dry bread
crumbs

Combine egg yolks and sugar and beat ½ hour by hand or ten minutes with the electric mixer. Add spices and dry bread crumbs and stir until blended. Carefully fold in stiffly beaten egg whites. Bake in buttered and crumbed tube pan at 325 degrees for one hour. (Do not open oven during baking time or cake will fall.) Invert pan to cool. To serve, sprinkle with powdered sugar.

KECKS
(Cookies)

While cakes and yeast breads were baked in the individual kitchens, bread was baked every day on the hearth in the bakery found in each village. Around Christmastime the fire to heat the oven was built just a bit higher so that there was enough heat left after the bread was done to bake the many fancy traditional cookies. Each family prepared its own dough and brought it to the bakery on the day assigned to them for baking. The cookie recipes called for lots of butter and eggs which may seem like an extravagance now but those were things of which there was an abundance then.

MARZIPAN
(White Sugar Marchpane Cookies)

8 eggs	1 teaspoon soda
4½ cups white sugar	½ teaspoon baking
8 cups flour	powder

Beat eggs until thick and light. Add sugar and beat again with rotary egg beater or electric mixer for 15 minutes. Add flour sifted with soda and baking powder. Place the dough on a floured board; taking part of it at a time, roll out to about quarter inch thickness. Cut into fancy shapes with cookie cutters. With rim of thimble or similar object, make some decorative, geometric impressions on top of cookies. Place the cut-out cookies on a towel-covered board overnight in a cool place. Place on greased cookie sheet and bake in 325 degree oven for 10 or 12 minutes. These cookies should **not** be browned, only nicely baked through. Store in tightly covered container.

BRAUNER ZUCKER MARZIPAN
(Brown Sugar Marchpane Cookies)

4 eggs, separated	4 cups sifted flour
2¼ cups firmly-packed	1 teaspoon soda
brown sugar	

Beat egg whites. Add beaten yolks and sugar and beat well. Add flour and soda. Handle dough lightly and roll out on floured board ¾ of an inch thick. Use as little flour as possible, just enough to avoid sticking to board. Cut into fancy shapes with cookie cutters and continue directions as in recipe above.

KOKOSNUSZ KECKS
(Coconut Cookies)

1½ cups butter
1½ cups brown sugar
1½ cups granulated
   sugar

6 eggs
½ lb. cocoanut
6 cups flour

1½ teaspoons baking powder

Cream butter, add sugar gradually, blending well. Add one egg at a time, beating after each addition. Add cocoanut, then flour sifted with baking powder. Drop by teaspoons onto greased baking sheet and bake in a moderate oven (375 degrees) about 15 minutes.

DATTEL KECKS
(Date Cookies)

2 eggs
1 cup sugar
1 cup flour
½ teaspoon baking
   powder

¼ teaspoon cinnamon
1 cup dates, chopped
1 cup nuts, chopped
Powdered sugar

Beat eggs and sugar. Sift together flour, baking powder and cinnamon and add. Fold in dates and nuts. Spread on greased baking sheet. Bake in 325 degree oven for 15 to 20 minutes. Cut into 1x2 inch bars and roll in powdered sugar.

❖❖❖❖❖❖❖❖❖❖❖❖❖❖❖❖❖❖❖❖❖❖❖❖❖❖❖❖❖❖❖❖❖❖❖❖
COOKIES
❖❖❖❖❖❖❖❖❖❖❖❖❖❖❖❖❖❖❖❖❖❖❖❖❖❖❖❖❖❖❖❖❖❖❖❖

LEBKUCHEN
(Honey Cookies)

2 tablespoons soda
1/4 cup brandy
1 quart honey
2 2/3 cups brown sugar
4 eggs, well-beaten

2 cups coarsely-
ground nuts
1/2 cup chopped can-
died citron peel
10 cups sifted flour

Dissolve soda in brandy. Heat the honey; remove from heat and add sugar. When cooled, add the well-beaten eggs, then the soda, nuts, citron peel, and flour. Let stand over night. Place dough on floured board and knead well. Taking part of it at a time, form into rolls about 2 inches in diameter and slice off the cookies one-fourth inch thick. Place on greased cookie sheet and bake in 350 degree oven for about ten minutes.

BUTTER PLÄTZCHEN
(Butter Cookies)

1 cup butter
2¼ cups sugar

4 eggs
4 cups sifted flour
½ teaspoon soda

Cream butter and sugar. Add eggs and beat 7 minutes by electric mixer or 15 minutes by hand. Add flour sifted with soda. Roll out on lightly floured board. Cut with cookie cutter into desired shapes. Place on greased baking sheet and bake in moderate oven (350 degrees) 12 to 15 minutes.

PFEFFER NÜSSE

(Pfeffer Nüsse)

1⅛ cup brown sugar, firmly packed
1⅛ cup granulated sugar
2 eggs
4 egg yolks

1 teaspoon soda
A pinch each of cinnamon, cloves and black pepper
4 cups all purpose flour, sifted

2 oz. candied citron, if desired

Mix first five ingredients and beat continuously for 15 minutes. Add spices and flour gradually, then citron if desired. Roll dough into small balls the size of English walnuts and let stand overnight in a dry, not too warm, place. Bake in 325 degree oven 20 to 25 minutes.

SCHÖPF KECKS
(Drop Cookies)

1 tablespoon butter
2¼ cups sugar
4 eggs

4 cups flour
1 teaspoon baking powder

Cream butter and sugar; add unbeaten eggs and mix well. Sift flour with baking powder and add to creamed mixture. Drop by teaspoons onto greased baking sheet. Bake in moderate oven (350 degrees) 12 to 15 minutes.

COOKIES

WIESBADER BROT
(Rolled Cookies)

½ cup butter
1 cup sugar
2 whole eggs
1 teaspoon cinnamon

2 cups sifted flour
½ teaspoon baking
  soda
1 egg yolk for topping

Cream butter and sugar until very light; add eggs and beat again until foamy. Then add flour sifted with cinnamon and soda. Chill. Roll out to quarter inch thickness; cut in oblong strips about 1 inch wide and 2 inches long. Place on greased baking sheet and brush with beaten egg yolk. Bake in slow oven, 325 degrees, for about 10 to 15 minutes.

KRUMMEN KECKS
(Crumb Cookies)

6 eggs
3 cups brown sugar
3 cups finely chopped
  nuts

3 cups dry coffee cake
  crumbs
2 heaping teaspoons
  baking powder

Beat eggs; add sugar and beat until thick. Add nuts, then crumbs mixed with the baking powder. Drop by teaspoons onto greased baking sheet and bake at 350 degrees for about ten minutes.

SCHOKOLADE KECKS No. 1
(Chocolate Cookies)

½ cup butter
2 cups brown sugar
5 eggs

4 oz. sweet chocolate
melted
4 cups flour

1 teaspoon soda

Cream butter, add sugar gradually. Beat in eggs one at a time. Add melted chocolate, then flour mixed with soda. Drop by teaspoons onto greased baking sheet and bake in 325 degree oven for 12 to 15 minutes.

SCHOKOLADE KECKS No. 2
(Chocolate Cookies)

6 egg whites, stiffly
beaten
2 cups sugar
½ cup chopped nut-
meats

8 oz. grated sweet
chocolate
2 tablespoons flour,
sifted
½ teaspoon baking
powder

Beat egg whites, add sugar gradually, then nuts, chocolate, and flour mixed with the baking powder. Blend well. Drop by teaspoons onto greased baking sheet and bake in moderate oven (350 degrees) 10 or 15 minutes.

✦✦✦
COOKIES
✦✦✦

ZWETCHEN KECKS
(Prune Drop Cookies)

2/3 cup butter
1 cup brown sugar
1 cup white sugar
2 well-beaten eggs
1 teaspoon vanilla
1/2 cup sour milk
1 teaspoon soda

1 cup chopped
   cooked prunes
3 1/2 cups flour
1 teaspoon baking
   powder
1 teaspoon cinna-
   mon

1/2 cup chopped nutmeats

Cream butter and sugar. Add the beaten eggs. Mix well.
Dissolve soda in milk and add with remaining ingredients.
Drop by teaspoons on greased cookie sheet. Bake 15 min-
utes in moderate oven, 350 degrees.

HAFER-FLOCKEN KECKS
(Oatmeal Cookies)

½ cup lard
2 cups sugar
2 eggs
2½ cups flour
2½ cups oatmeal

1 teaspoon soda
4 tablespoons sour milk
1 teaspoon vanilla
1 cup raisins, if desired

Cream lard, add sugar and mix well. Add one egg at a time
and beat well after each addition. Add flour, oatmeal and
soda alternately with milk and vanilla. Add raisins if desired. Drop by teaspoons onto greased baking sheet and
bake in moderate oven (350 degrees) for 12 to 15 minutes.

✤✤
AMANA COLONY RECIPES
✤✤

OSTER HASEN
(Easter Bunnies)

1⅛ cups brown sugar,
  firmly packed
1⅛ cups granulated sugar
4 large eggs
4 cups sifted flour

¼ teaspoon baking powder
¼ teaspoon baking soda
2 or 3 tablespoons melted
  butter or other
  shortening

Beat eggs, add sugars and beat with electric mixer at high speed for five minutes. Gradually add dry ingredients which have been sifted together. Add melted shortening and roll out on floured board to about ⅜ inch thickness. Cut with bunny-shaped or other fancy cookie cutter and bake on greased cookie sheet at 350 degrees for 15 or 20 minutes.

MANDEL KECKS
(Almond Cookies)

6 egg yolks
1⅛ cup sugar
½ lb. finely ground
  almonds

1 cup flour
1 teaspoon baking
  powder

Beat egg yolks; add sugar and almonds and blend well. Add flour sifted with baking powder. Roll out on lightly floured board and cut with cookie cutter into desired shapes. Place on greased cookie sheet and bake in 325 degree oven for 12 to 15 minutes.

❖❖❖❖❖❖❖❖❖❖❖❖❖❖❖❖❖❖❖❖❖❖❖❖❖❖❖❖❖❖❖❖❖❖❖❖❖❖
COOKIES
❖❖❖❖❖❖❖❖❖❖❖❖❖❖❖❖❖❖❖❖❖❖❖❖❖❖❖❖❖❖❖❖❖❖❖❖❖❖

NUSS PLÄTZCHEN
(Nut Cookies)

6 egg whites
2¼ cups sugar
Dash of cinnamon

2 cups finely chopped filberts or hazelnuts
2 cups flour

1 teaspoon baking powder

Beat egg whites until stiff; gradually add sugar and cinnamon and stir until well blended. Add nuts and flour sifted with baking powder. Drop by teaspoons onto greased baking sheet and bake in 325 degree oven for 12 to 15 minutes.

BLASEN CONFEKT
(Kisses)

1¾ cups powdered sugar

½ cup almonds, ground

1 egg white, stiffly beaten

Fold sugar and almonds into beaten egg white and drop by teaspoons onto cookie sheet lined with oiled paper. Bake 15 minutes in 300 degree oven.

MAKRONEN
(Macaroons)

6 egg whites
2 cups sugar

4 cups cocoanut
4 tablespoons flour

Beat egg whites, add sugar gradually, then cocoanut and flour. Drop by teaspoons onto greased baking sheet. Bake in 325 degree oven 12 to 15 minutes.

GETRÄNKE
(Beverages)

Fruit juices were one of the few things prepared at home and were considered quite a treat. One of the more unusual was concocted from orange rinds. Oranges were seldom had since they were not grown at home; but at Christmastime each child was sure to find one under the tree. The fruit was peeled very thin to include as little of the membrane as possible, then the peelings were packed in a glass jar, covered with vinegar and sealed. In the summer a little of the orange-vinegar was put in a glass, some sugar added, then filled with water. It was a pleasant contrast to the sweeter juices made from cherries and grapes.

JOHANNISBEER SAFT
(Currant Juice)

2 cups vinegar
4 cups water
1 gallon currants

Sugar—2 cups to each
pint of juice

Wash currants, put into large mixing bowl. Pour vinegar and water over currants and let stand for five hours. Press and strain, add two cups of sugar for each pint of juice and boil rapidly for fifteen minutes. Fill into sterilized bottles or jars. Seal, and store in cool place. To serve, use one-fourth cup of the juice for each glass of water. Stir well and serve ice-cold.

KIRSCHEN SAFT
(Cherry Juice)

2 gallons cherries

Sugar—2 cups per pint
of juice

Wash and stem cherries. Mash in a large bowl and let stand for twelve hours. Then strain through jelly bag. To each pint of strained juice, add two cups of sugar. Put into preserving kettle and simmer for fifteen minutes. Fill into sterilized bottles and seal. To serve, dilute ¼ cup juice with 1 cup water.

TRAUBEN SAFT
(Grape Juice)

2 cups water   3 quarts grapes, washed

Sugar, 1 cup per quart of juice

Heat water and grapes to boiling. Cook slowly for 20 minutes. Filter through jelly bag. Measure juice and add one cup of sugar for each quart of juice. Bring to boil. Pour into sterilized bottles or jars and seal. To serve, dilute with equal amount of water.

EIER PUNCH
(Egg Punch)

1½ quarts red wine   Juice of 1 lemon
1 quart water   Nutmeg and cloves to
1⅛ cups sugar   taste

8 eggs, beaten

Combine all ingredients except eggs and heat. Add beaten eggs and continue beating until frothy on top. Do not boil or mixture will curdle. Serve at once.

GLÜH WEIN
(Hot Wine)

2 cups red wine   6 cloves
1⅛ cups sugar   ½ stick cinnamon

Heat to boiling point and serve immediately.

❖❖

BEVERAGES

❖❖

GEKÄNTES OBST UND GEMÜSE
(Canned Fruits and Vegetables)

Fall climaxed the busy summer of canning and storing for winter. The long shelves in the kitchen basement were loaded with the many, many jars of canned fruits and vegetables, some leafy vegetables and roots were stored in sand, huge vats of sauerkraut stood about in the corners, and in the attic were hung the bags of home-dried fruits. What hours of work in growing, harvesting, and preparing were represented by these supplies, but, oh, the security all this provender gave against the long winter!

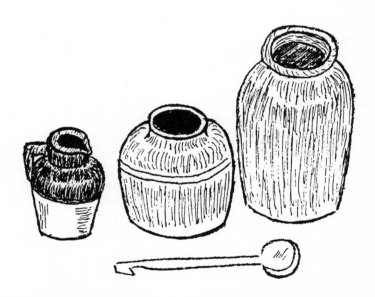

CHILI SAUCE No. 1
(Chili Sauce)

1 peck ripe tomatoes
6 green peppers
6 large onions
½ tablespoon cloves

1 tablespoon cinnamon
2 tablespoons salt
2 cups sugar
2 cups vinegar

Put tomatoes, peppers and onions through food chopper, using coarse blade. Add rest of ingredients and boil until quite thick. Fill into sterilized jars and seal.

CHILI SAUCE No. 2
(Chili Sauce)

9 large tomatoes
1 large onion
2 red peppers
1 teaspoon celery salt

1 tablespoon salt
½ cup vinegar
½ teaspoon cinnamon
1 cup sugar

Chop the vegetables fine. Add salts and vinegar and cook slowly for three hours, stirring frequently. Add cinnamon and sugar. Pour into sterilized pint jars and seal.

CHILI SAUCE No. 3
(Chili Sauce)

20 ripe tomatoes
3 large onions
2 green peppers
1 cup sugar

2 cups vinegar
3 tablespoons salt
1 teaspoon allspice
1 teaspoon cloves

1 teaspoon cinnamon

Put tomatoes, onions, and peppers through food chopper, using coarse blade. Add other ingredients in order given, and simmer slowly for one hour. Pour into sterilized jars and seal.

CATSUP
(Catsup)

1 gallon tomato juice
1 cup sugar
¼ cup salt
1 teaspoon mixed
   spices
1 teaspoon celery seed

¼ teaspoon pepper
1 small onion
1 clove garlic
2 tablespoons dry
   mustard
Vinegar

Bring tomato juice to boil, add sugar and salt. Tie spices into a cheesecloth bag and add. Tie onion and garlic into a separate bag and add. Lastly, add mustard mixed with enough vinegar to make a paste. Boil three hours or until thick. Pour into sterilized jars or bottles and seal.

CANNED FRUITS AND VEGETABLES

EINGEMACHTE TOMATEN SUPPE
(Canned Tomato Soup)

14 qts. sliced tomatoes	1 tablespoon celery seed
2 bay leaves	1 teaspoon soda
1 bunch parsley	1 cup flour
7 medium-sized onions,	6 tablespoons salt
sliced	½ tablespoon red pepper

1 cup sugar

Combine first six ingredients and cook until tedner. Put through sieve. Make a thin paste of the flour with some of the tomato juice. Add this and remaining ingredients to the tomato juice and cook slowly for half an hour. Fill into sterilized jars and seal.

To serve, dilute with milk or cream to desired consistency.

SAUERE GRÜNE SCHNITTBOHNEN
(Sour Green Beans)

Green string beans, thinly sliced length-wise	4½ cups water
	½ cup vinegar
	¼ cup salt

Blanch sliced beans and pack into glass jars. Combine water, vinegar and salt in above proportions, bring to boil and pour over beans, filling jar. Seal.

Prepare according to recipe given in vegetable section; not eaten as a relish.

✦✧✦✧✦✧✦✧✦✧✦✧✦✧✦✧✦✧✦✧✦✧✦✧✦✧✦✧✦✧✦✧✦✧✦✧✦✦
AMANA COLONY RECIPES
✦✧✦✧✦✧✦✧✦✧✦✧✦✧✦✧✦✧✦✧✦✧✦✧✦✧✦✧✦✧✦✧✦✧✦✧✦✦

SÜSZ-SAUERE GRÜNE TOMATEN No. 1
(Pickled Green Tomatoes)

1 peck small green
   tomatoes, sliced
1 dozen small onions,
   peeled and sliced
1 small red pepper,
   minced

½ cup salt
2¼ cups sugar
4 cups vinegar
1 tablespoon mustard
   seed

Mix first four ingredients and let stand three hours. Drain.
Add sugar, vinegar and mustard seed and cook until tomatoes are tender. Fill into sterilized jars and seal.

SÜSZ-SAUERE GRÜNE TOMATEN No. 2
(Pickled Green Tomatoes)

4 lbs. green tomatoes,
   washed and sliced
½ cup salt

Vinegar to cover
4½ cups sugar
½ teaspoon cinnamon

Mix tomatoes and salt and let stand overnight. Drain. Add
vinegar to cover and let stand one hour. Drain again, saving 1 pint of the vinegar. Bring vinegar and sugar to boil,
add drained tomatoes and cook until tender. Remove tomatoes and cook syrup until thick. Return tomatoes to syrup,
add cinnamon, and bring again to boil. Fill into sterilized
jars and seal.

❖❖

CANNED FRUITS AND VEGETABLES

❖❖

SÜSZ-SAUERE ZWIEBEL
(Sweet-sour Onions)

3 cups pickle onions
Salt water to cover
2/3 cup vinegar

2 tablespoons sugar
2 cups water
2 teaspoons salt

Scald onions, peel, then boil in salt water until tender. Drain. Boil remaining ingredients together for five minutes. Then add onions and bring to a rolling boil. Cool and serve as a relish. May also be filled into sterilized jars and kept for future use.

SÜSZ-SAUERES OBST
(Pickled Fruit)

7 lbs. prepared fruit (pears, apples, citron, plums or ground cherries)
3½ lbs. sugar
1 pint vinegar

1 stick cinnamon
6 cloves

Boil all ingredients together until fruit is tender. Skim out fruit and boil syrup 20 minutes. Return fruit to syrup, let simmer several minutes longer. Fill into sterilized jars and seal.

EINGEMACHTE SÜSZ-SAUERE EIER
(Pickled Eggs)

8 or 10 hard-boiled
eggs
1¾ cups vinegar
1¼ cups water
3 tablespoons sugar

2 teaspoons celery seed
1 small red hot pepper
1 tablespoon mustard
seed
Pinch of mace

Peel eggs and pack tightly into quart jar. Combine remaining ingredients in saucepan and boil for five minutes. Pour boiling hot over eggs in jar and seal. Ready to eat in four or five days. Should be kept in refrigerator after opening.

SÜSZ-SAUERE ROTERÜBEN
(Pickled Beets)

2 quarts beets, prepared
as directed
2 cups sugar

2 cups vinegar
2 cups water
2 teaspoons salt, if desired

Boil beets until tender, dip into cold water, peel and quarter. Combine remaining ingredients, bring to boil; add beets and bring to boil again. Fill into sterilized jars and seal.

CANNED FRUITS AND VEGETABLES

DILL MIX
(Dill Mix)

3 qts. yellow beans,
  whole
3 qts. scraped carrots,
  whole
3 qts. small pickle on-
  ions, peeled

2 qts. water
½ cup salt
½ cup vinegar
Dill

Boil vegetables separately until tender but not too soft. Then combine with water, salt and vinegar and bring to boil. Fill into sterilized jars, put 1 head of dill in top of each, and seal.

KATER BOHNEN
(Dill Beans)

Yellow string beans
4½ cups water

½ cup vinegar
¼ cup salt

Dill

Wash beans, string, and cook in salted water until tender. Drain. Combine water, vinegar and salt in above propor-tions, bring to boil and pour over beans which have been packed into glass jars. Put a head of dill in top of jar and seal.

GUMMER FISCHLEIN
(Cucumber Fishes)

2 quarts large cucum-
bers, peeled and
sliced lengthwise
½ cup salt

1½ cups vinegar
1½ cups sugar
1½ cups water
1 head dill

Combine cucumbers and salt and let stand in earthen crock or bowl for 2 hours. Drain. Bring vinegar, sugar and water to boil and pour over cucumbers. Add dill. Ready to serve in two days.

GURKEN
(Pickles)

2 quarts small cucum-
bers
2 cups sugar

2 cups vinegar
1½ cups water
Dill, if desired

Wash cucumbers and soak in brine overnight; rinse in clear water. Combine sugar, vinegar and water and bring to boil. Add cucumbers and bring to boil again. When cucumbers have changed color, fill into sterilized jars, add dill (if desired) and seal.

CANNED FRUITS AND VEGETABLES

SACHSEN GUMMERN
(Dill Pickles in Jars)

Cucumbers, enough to fill 2-quart jar	Dill
Grape leaves	½ cup salt
Cherry leaves	1 cup vinegar
	Water

Wash cucumbers and fit into jar. Add several grape leaves and cherry leaves and several heads of dill. Dissolve salt in vinegar and pour over cucumbers. Add enough cold water to fill jar. Seal.

SCHMIERKÄSE
(Cheese Spread)

4 cups dry cottage cheese	1 tablespoon butter
1 teaspoon soda	1 tablespoon salt
	1 cup sweet cream

Put all ingredients together in top of double boiler and cook until melted. Remove from heat and add 1 teaspoon caraway seed for seasoning, if desired. Store in cool place.

MENUS

These menus are not offered as suggestions, they are merely listed to give an example of the kinds of meals served. The general pattern was followed week after week, Tuesday was "Mehlspeis" day, Wednesday meant boiled beef, Thursday promised a special dessert, etc. Certain meals were the same each week. For instance, Saturday's supper was always cottage cheese and potatoes boiled with the jackets on, Sunday's breakfast boasted coffee cake instead of the usual fried potatoes. Instead of seeming monotonous, this schedule proved very convenient for the cook who this way always had a ready answer to "what shall I cook today?"

A WEEK'S DINNER MENUS FOR WINTER SEASON

Riebel Soup
Boiled Spare Ribs
Fried Round Potatoes
Sour Beans and Navy Beans
Amana Coffee Cake

Cream Soup
Roast Beef
Potato Dumplings with Onion Sauce
Cabbage Salad
Apple Sauce

Rice Soup
Boiled Beef
Horseradish Sauce
Raw Fried Potatoes
Colony Cabbage
Spiced Plums
Pie

Dumpling Soup
Meat Patties
Mashed Potatoes with Browned Crumbs
Red Cabbage
Baked Apples
Spice Cake

Potato Soup
Boiled Pork
Whipped Potatoes
Sauerkraut
Chili Sauce
Cookies

Browned Crumb Soup
Bacon and Eggs
Potatoes in Sauce
Leftover Sauerkraut
Stewed Dried Apples
Sweet Yeastbread Buns

A WEEK'S DINNER MENUS FOR SUMMER SEASON

Cotton Soup
Roast Pork
Boiled Potatoes
Peas
Head Lettuce
Streusel Kuchen

Pea Soup
Breaded Pork Loin
Creamed Potatoes
Cole Slaw
Waffles with Strawberries

Vegetable Soup
Sliced Boiling Beef (used
    for making soup stock)
Fried Potatoes
Spinach
Radish Salad
Rhubarb Kuchen

Dumpling Soup
Sauerbraten
Parsley Potatoes
Carrots
Pickled Beets
Cookies

Farina Soup
Pork Loin Roast
Boiled Potatoes
Cauliflower
Tomato Salad
Canned Fruit

Tomato Soup
Liver Dumplings
Boiled Potatoes
Lettuce
Apple Sauce

A WEEK'S EVENING MEAL MENUS

Amana Pork Sausage
Boiled Potatoes
Horseradish Sauce
Endive Salad

Meat Patties
Crumbed Potatoes
Cucumber Salad
Stewed Apples with Raisins

Breaded Bacon
Boiled Potatoes
Navy Beans
Pickled Beets

Ham Salad
Crumbed Potatoes
Pickled Onions
Cornbread with Syrup

Scrambled Ham and Eggs
Creamed Potatoes
Celery Salad

Pork Rind Sausage
Hot Potato Salad
Fried Eggs
Dill Pickles

Pork Crackles
Potatoes boiled in jackets
Cottage Cheese
Green Onions or Chives

Schmierkäse

SPECIAL OCCASION MENUS

New Year's

Noodle Soup
Breaded Pork
Mashed Potatoes
Salsify
Spiced Citron
New Year's Pretzel

Easter

Dumpling Soup
Ham
Mashed Potatoes
Asparagus
Leaf Lettuce
Rice Pudding
Canned Peaches

Thanksgiving

Chicken
Mashed Potatoes
Red Cabbage
Spiced Citron
Apple Kuchen

Christmas

Rice Soup
Creamed Chicken
Noodles
Mashed Potatoes
Cole Slaw
Stewed Prunes and Peaches

RECEPTER INHALTSVERZEICHNIS

RECIPE INDEX